Look at the garden

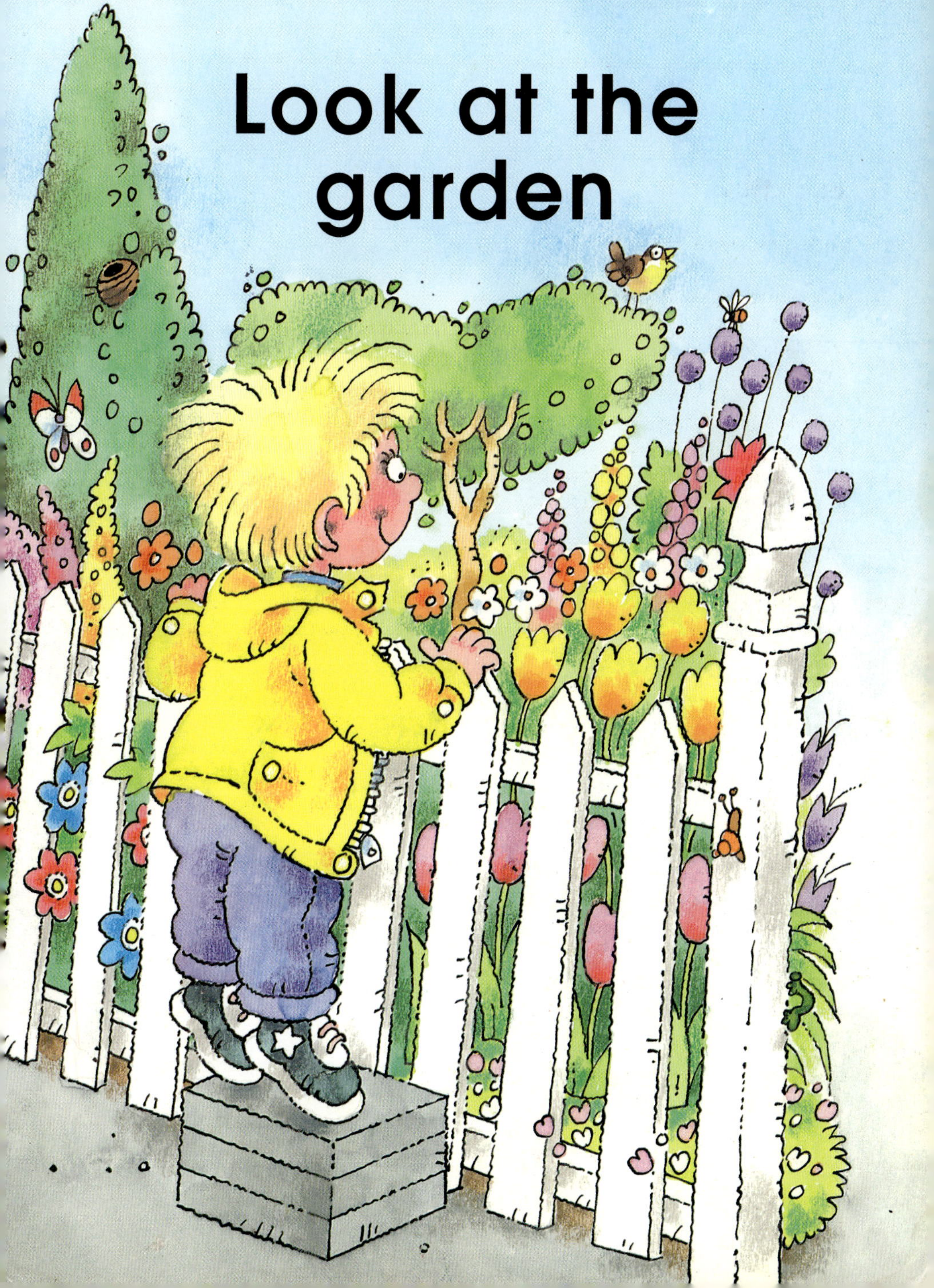

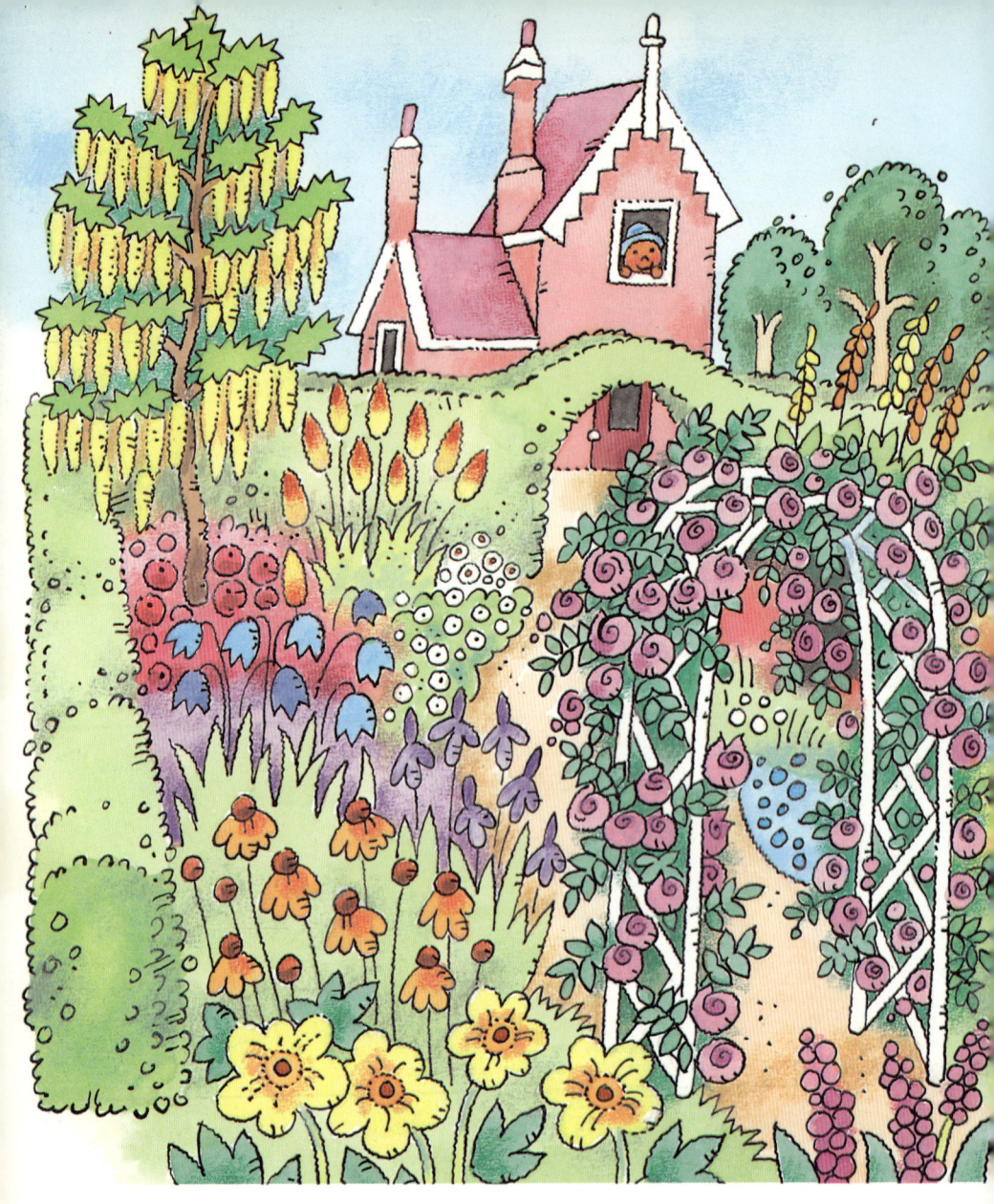

We see flowers in the garden.

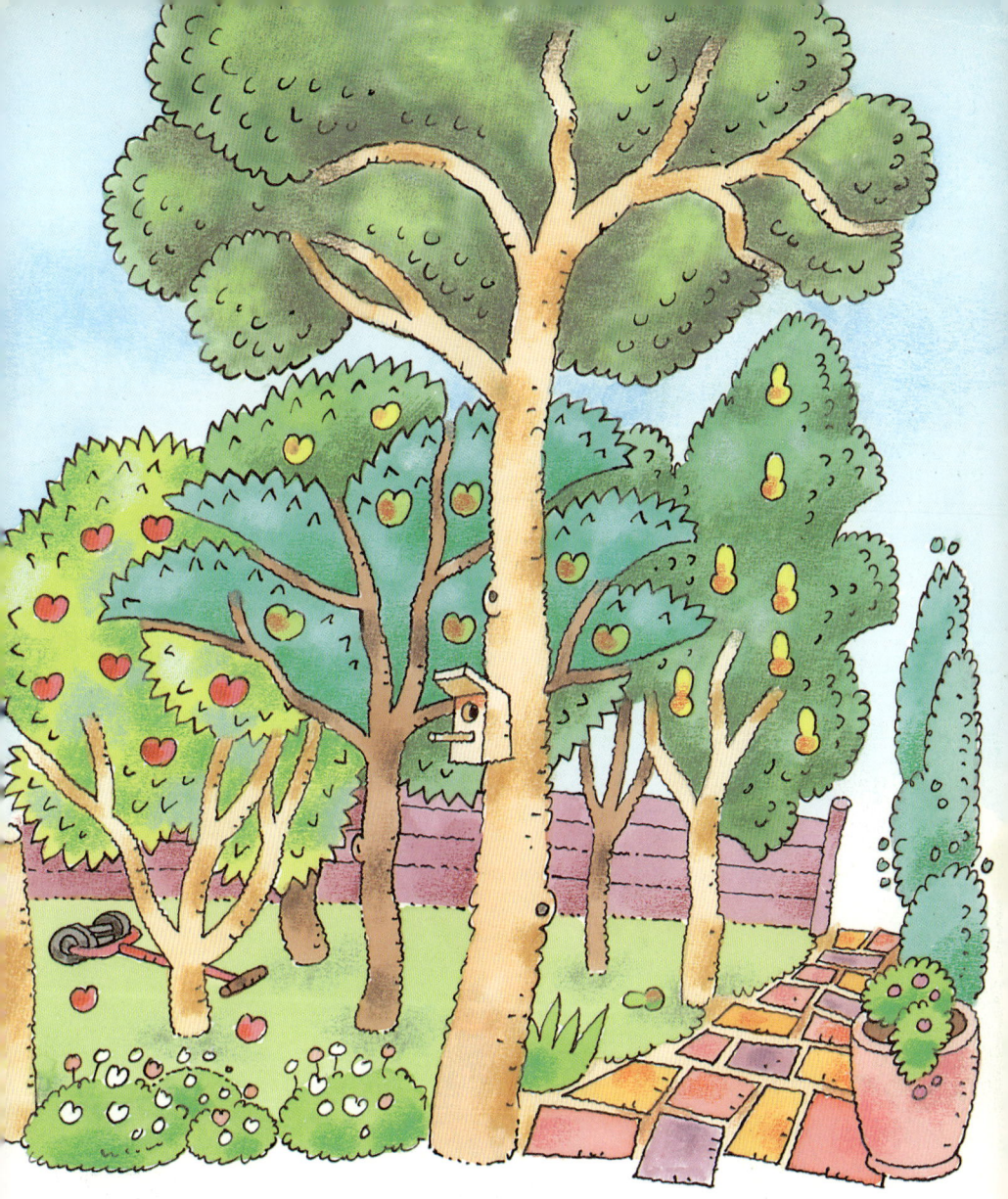

We see trees in the garden.

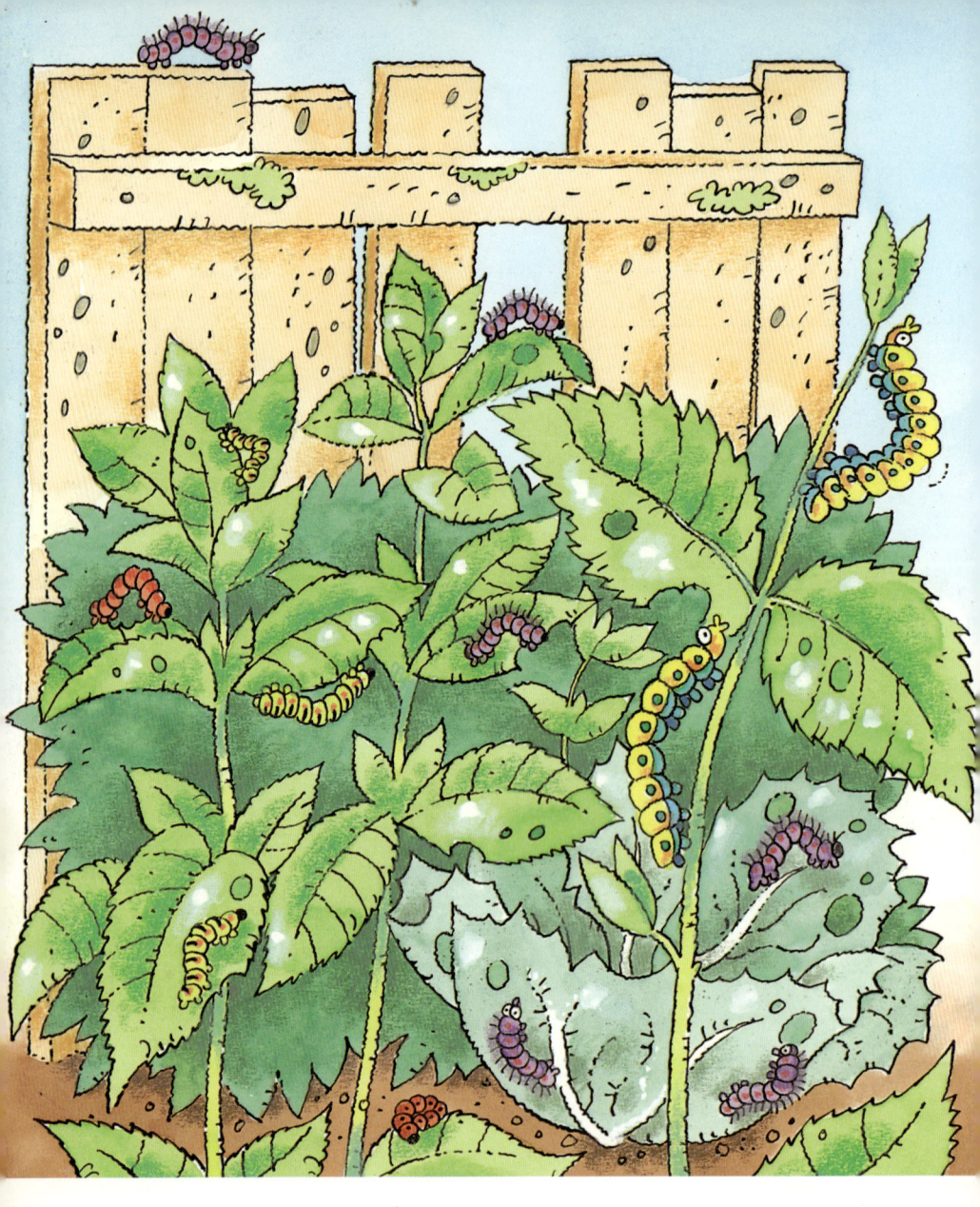

We see caterpillars in the garden.

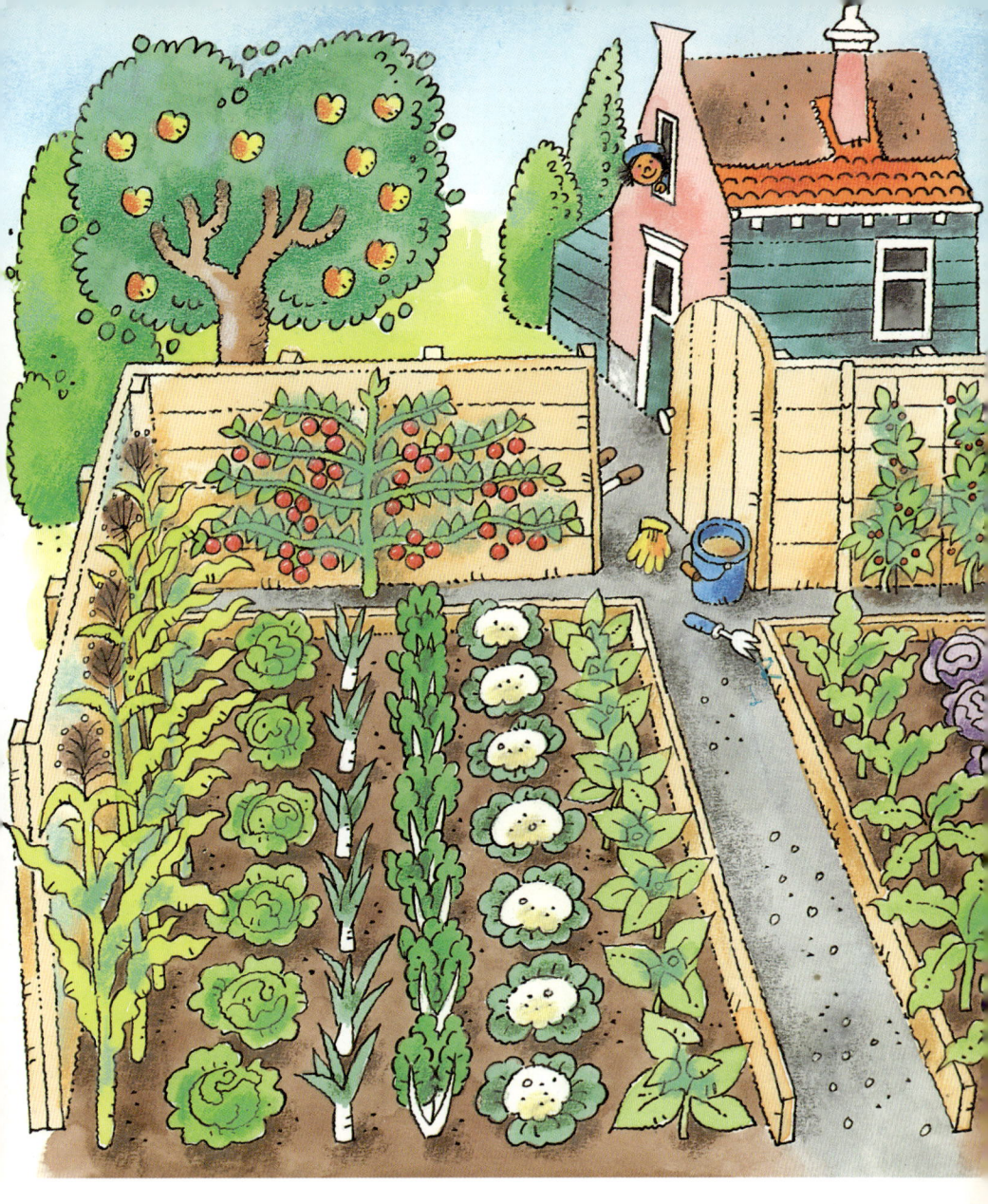

We see vegetables in the garden.

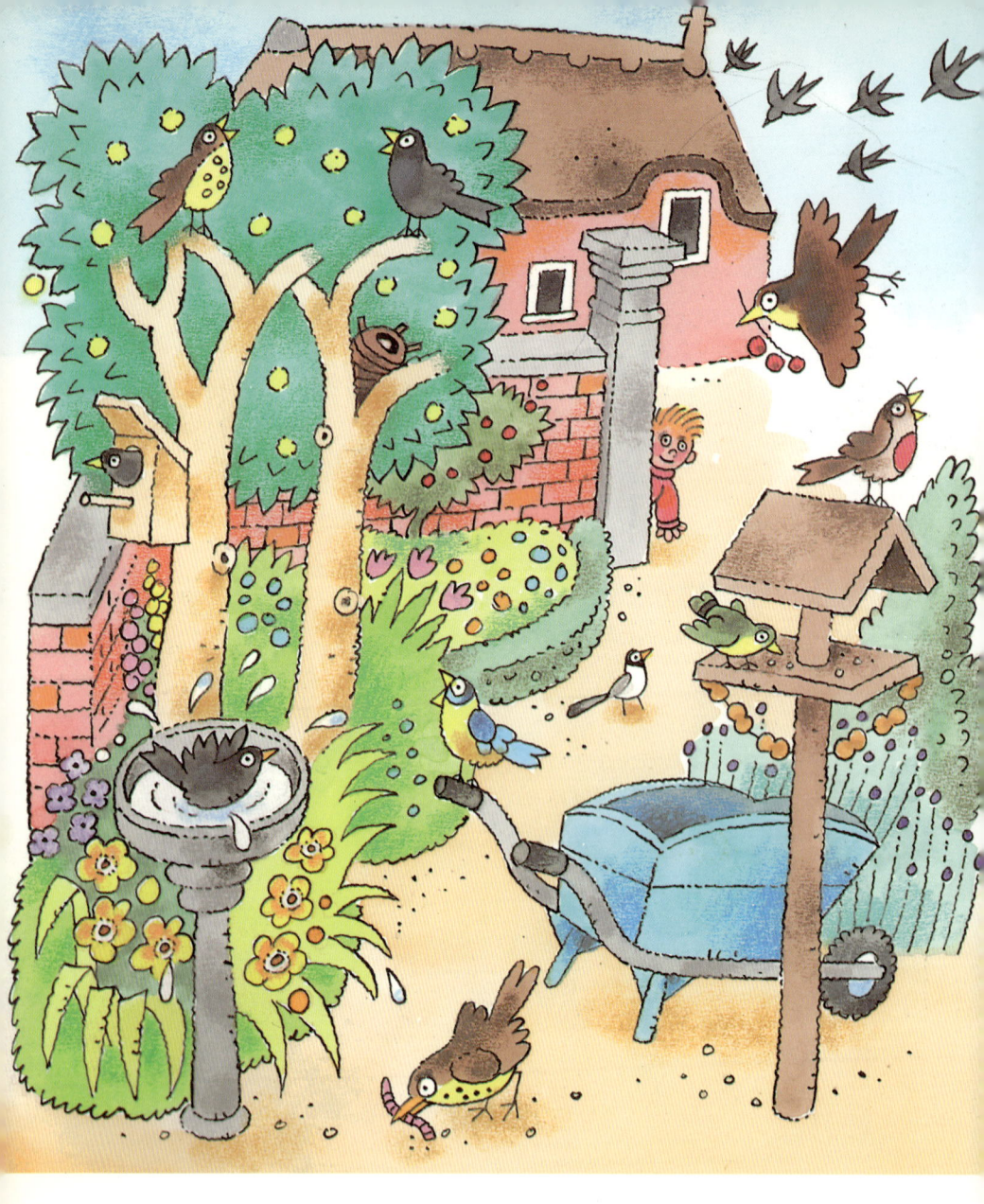

We see birds in the garden.

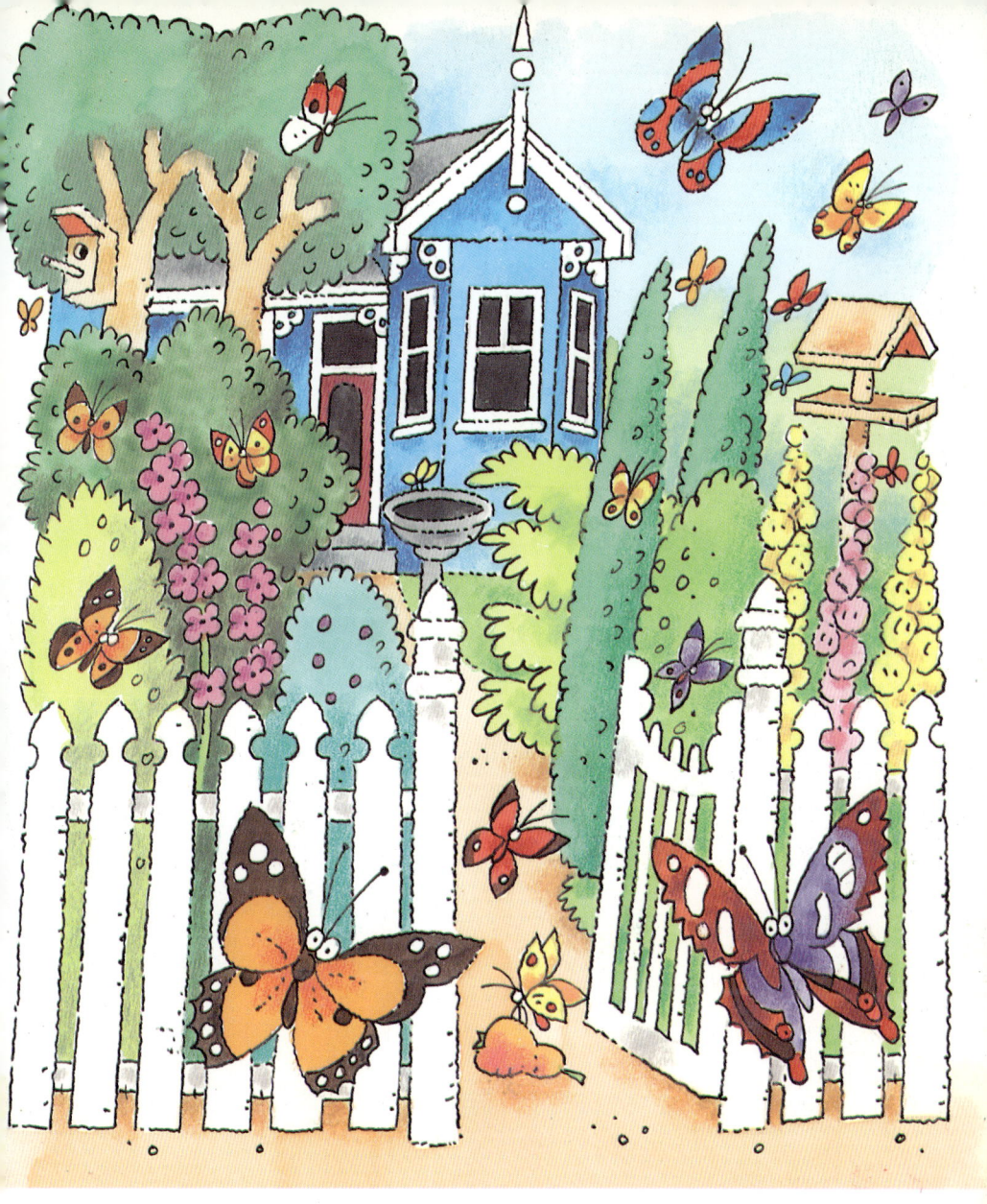

We see butterflies in the garden.

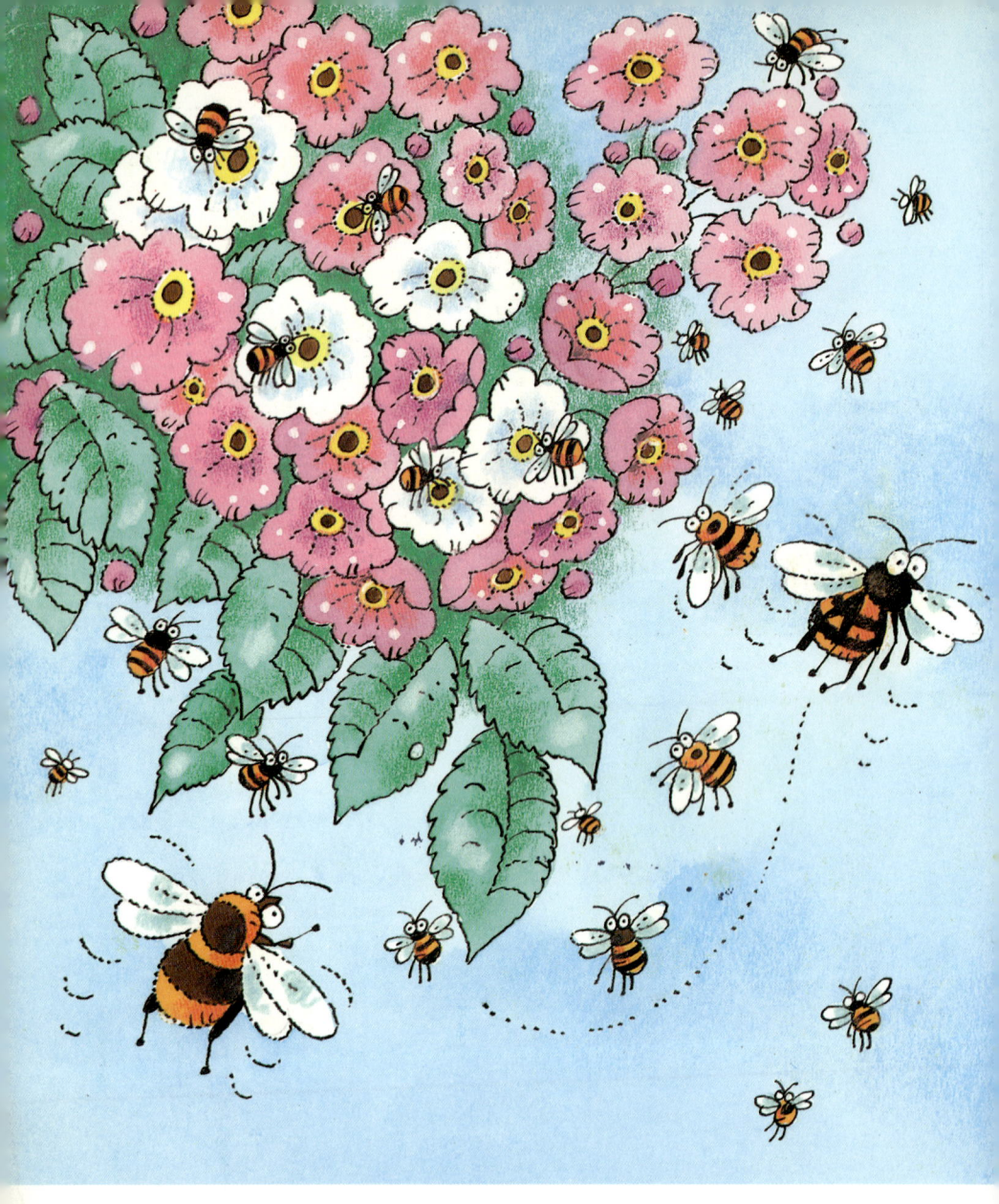

We see bees in the garden. Buzzzzz!